Contents

Spiders' bodies

Spiders live all over the world. There are thousands of different sorts, but they all have the same shaped body. Have a look next time you see one.

The crab spider is as small as your little fingernail.

The Goliath tarantula is as big as a frisbee.

What are spiders?

Spiders are members of an animal family called arachnids. They can be big or small, but they all have eight legs.

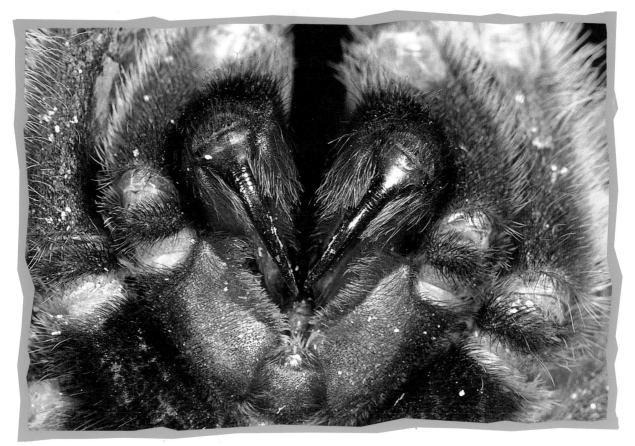

A spider's fangs are poisonous and sharp.

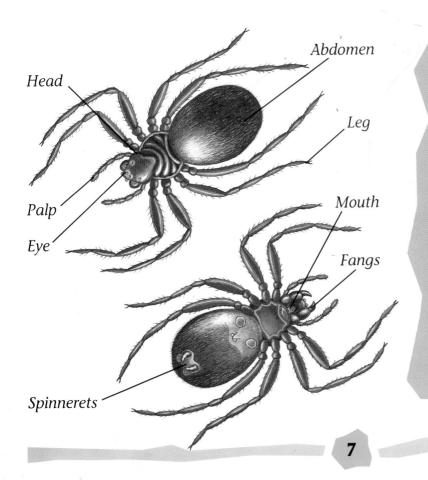

Head

Abdomen

Leg

Palp

Eye

Mouth

Fangs

Spinnerets

Spidery parts
A spider's body is split into two parts – the head and the abdomen.

On the head are its legs, its fangs and two palps. Palps help the spider to taste and feel.

On the abdomen are spinnerets, which make silk for spinning webs.

Spider skin

Spiders have a tough coat that protects their bodies and gives them their shape. This thick coat is called the exoskeleton.

Total cover
The exoskeleton covers every part of a spider's body, even its eyes.

The Chilean rose tarantula has a hairy body. All spiders have some hairs on their body.

Shedding skin

❶ The exoskeleton that a spider starts life with does not grow with the spider. In time, it begins to feel tight and splits open.

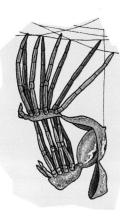

❷ The spider pulls itself out of the old skin. Underneath is a new, larger skin.

❸ The spider's new skin is soft like jelly. It takes a few hours to harden in the air.

Unwanted coat

As soon as the spider's skin has hardened, the spider scuttles away leaving its old coat behind. The picture below is of an empty old spider skin.

Spider silk

Spiders dangle from a thread that is finer than hair, but much stronger and very stretchy. The thread is called silk. Spiders use silk to make their webs, tie up their prey and protect their eggs.

Silk oozes out of the spinnerets. Spiders pull it out with their legs to make long, hard threads.

Spiders use their webs to catch insects. As soon as an insect flies into a web, the spider feels the silk shake.

Making a web

The orb spider spins a round web. You often see it in gardens.

A spider's web is a deadly trap for catching flies and other insects. The fine, lacy threads are soon spoilt by dust, rain or gusts of wind, so most spiders spin a new web each night. Webs take about an hour to make.

❶ The spider makes a strong thread between two twigs.

❷ Then it makes a second, looser thread and pulls it down.

Not all webs are round. This one is triangle-shaped and is found in the grass. It is made by the money spider.

❸ The spider adds more spokes and fixes them firmly.

❹ A final, sticky, spiral thread holds all the spokes in place.

Catching a meal

When an insect flies into a spider's web, it gets stuck in the sticky threads. The spider dashes over, bites the insect with its poisonous fangs, then wraps it up tightly in silk. A spider often saves its meals for later.

A spider waits in its web for an insect to land. It keeps very still.

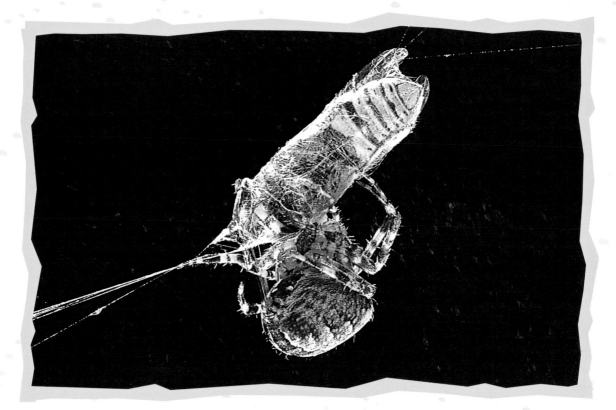

A garden spider wraps up a wasp. A spider can store several insect meals in its web.

Spider soup

Spiders have such small mouths that they can only eat food that is runny. The poison they inject into their prey changes its body to a kind of soup, which the spider can then suck up.

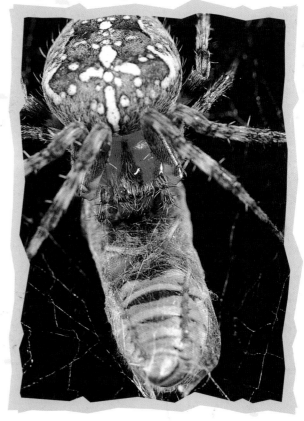

Hunters

Many spiders do not spin webs; they hunt for their food instead. Hunting spiders are strong and fast, and have good eyesight to spot their prey.

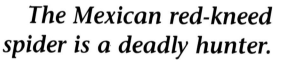

The Mexican red-kneed spider is a deadly hunter.

Long jumper

The zebra spider has two huge eyes that help it to spot tiny creatures and work out how far it must jump to catch them. The spider pounces and pins them down, then bites them with its fangs.

Silk shooter

The bolas spider hunts for its food by throwing out a line of sticky silk. It swings the silk round like a cowboy's lasso to catch insects as they fly by.

Poison spitter

The spitting spider stalks its prey like a cat. When the spider gets close, it fires a sticky poison from its fangs, pinning its meal to the ground.

Big hunter

Most tarantula spiders eat insects, but some also track down and kill larger animals, such as frogs, lizards, snakes and chicks!

Hiding

Some spiders are sneaky hunters. They ambush their prey. They hide somewhere safe and lie in wait for an insect. As soon as a tasty meal comes near, they jump out and grab it – fast!

Under the ground

Some spiders hide under the ground to ambush their prey. The trapdoor spider makes a burrow with a trapdoor on the top. At night, it opens the door a crack to keep a look-out for passing insects.

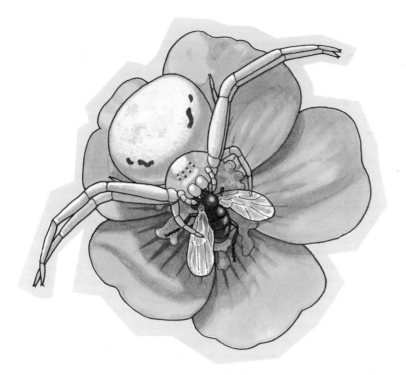

Inside a flower

The crab spider hides inside flowers where it catches visiting insects. The insects do not see the spider because it can change its colour to match the flower. The spider also keeps very still.

Behind a screen

The purse-web spider makes a silk tube on the ground, and covers it with bits of soil. The spider then hides inside the tube. It stabs passing insects through the soft, silk wall and drags them inside the tube.

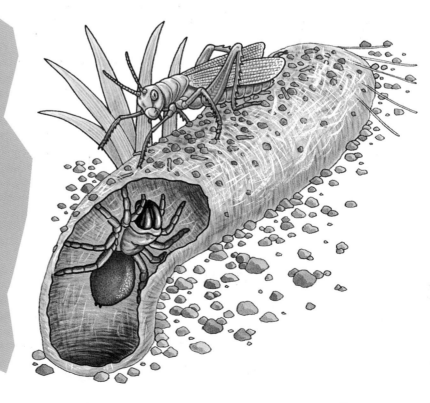

Finding a mate

A male spider must find a female mate to produce spiderlings – their young. To attract a female, the male spider may give her an insect, strum her web or wave his legs about. If she accepts him, the two spiders mate.

A male spider takes care as he is smaller than the female.

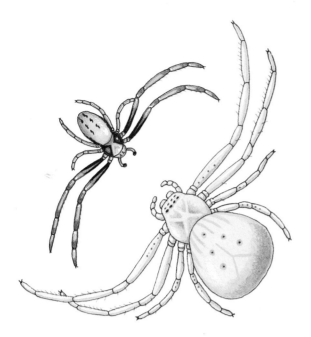

During mating, the male has to take care because the female is usually bigger than him and she may eat him by mistake!

A week or two after mating, the female lays her eggs in a soft bag of silk called a sac.

A female garden spider lays her eggs in a silk sac. She dies soon afterwards.

Spiderlings

Most female spiders leave their egg sacs on fences or trees. Next spring, the eggs hatch out into tiny spiderlings. The spiderlings need to spread out to find food. They each make a line of silk and float away on the breeze.

Egg carriers

Unlike most spiders, the nursery web spider does not leave her egg sac behind. She carries it around with her until the eggs hatch.

These spiderlings have just hatched out of their sac. Soon each one will go its own way. ▶

Escaping danger

Spiders make a juicy meal for all sorts of animals such as birds, lizards, toads and wasps. Most spiders escape from danger by dropping down on a line of silk. Others face their enemies, and go into the attack!

Dance defence
Hunting wasps are a wolf spider's greatest enemy, as they dig up the burrows where the spider hides. When it sees an enemy, the spider rises up on its legs and bares its fangs.

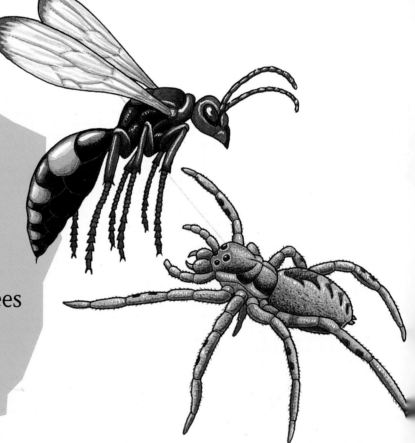

Hair attack

A bird-eating spider attacks its enemies by brushing its hair on to them. The spider's hairs have sharp little hooks. These stick into the enemy's skin and make it feel itchy and sore.

Spidery snippets

Spiders can be dangerous. In some places, they kill more people than snakes.

A black widow spider is about 15 times more poisonous than a rattlesnake.

A spider can go without food for several months.

The remains of ancient spiders have been found inside drops of sticky sap.

About 300 years ago, a Frenchman used spider silk to make stockings and gloves.

Spiders are ancient creatures. The first ones lived on Earth about 400 million years ago.

A jumping spider can leap 40 times the length of its body. That is like a person jumping the length of three tennis courts.

The web of the golden orb spider measures 2 metres across; some people use it as a fishing net.

Spiders are a farmer's friend. They eat many harmful insects.

Scientists are trying to find a way of making a poison just like a spider's. This could then be used on farm crops to kill harmful insects, without harming birds or the soil.

There may be 1000 spider eggs in an egg sac the size of a pea.

A jumping spider's eyes are bigger than its brain.

Glossary

Abdomen   The back part of the spider's body.

Arachnid   An animal, such as the spider, that has eight legs, two parts to the body and an exoskeleton.

Exoskeleton   The hard, outer coat that protects the body of spiders and many other animals.

Fangs   The sharp claws on a spider's head. Spiders use their fangs to bite and poison their prey.

Insect   One of a group of animals which all have six legs and three parts to their bodies.

Palp   A feeler on a spider's head that helps it to taste and feel. Spiders have two palps.

Prey   An animal that is hunted by another for food.

Sac   The bag of silk in which a female spider lays her eggs.

Spinneret   One of several small tubes on a spider, which squirt out the silk for making webs.

Index